My Soul is a Witness

A Little "Pocket" Book of Inspiration

by Ani

ISBN 0-9745129-0-7

RIM Books
P.O. Box 311825
Atlanta, GA   30331

Cover design by Jill Connolly

Printed in the United States by Morris Publishing
3212 East Highway 30
Kearney, NE 68847
1-800-650-7888

~ † ~

Psalm 100

HOLY BIBLE
KING JAMES VERSION

Make a joyful noise unto the Lord, all ye lands. [2]Serve the Lord with gladness: come before his presence with singing. [3]Know ye that the Lord he is God: it is he that hath made us, and not we ourselves: We are his people, and the sheep of his pasture. [4]Enter into his gates with thanksgiving, and into his courts with praise: be thankful unto him, and bless his name. [5]For the Lord is good; his mercy is everlasting; and his truth endureth to all generations.

~

~ † ~

Dedication

This book is dedicated to GOD, our Heavenly Father…

My strength and my salvation, without whom
this would have been impossible.

And to

My husband Robert and my son Mark,
My life, my love, my inspiration…..

THANK YOU FOR YOUR SUPPORT!

~

~ † ~

Introduction

During these trying times, we all need something to believe in, and to hold on to. In some small way, I hope the poems and verses on the following pages will be a form of inspiration that will help get you through some of those times.

"My Soul Is A Witness" was written with a focus on GOD, our heavenly Father. Whenever I feel discouraged, and my soul needs lifting, I know that I can call on Him and He will always be there.

At times, when I become impatient, I know that even though He may not come when I think He should, He's always on time – He's never late!

The following are original inspirational verses by Ani.

~

Inspirations

My Soul Is A Witness

Yes, I know that GOD is real –
Because my soul is a witness.

He'll fight your battles if you just keep still –
And, my soul is a witness.

He can light up even your darkest hour –
Yes, my soul is a witness.

Just trust in GOD, He's got staying power –
Truly, my soul is a witness.

If you put your trust in Him and never doubt –
My soul is a witness.

No matter the problem, He'll bring you out –
By faith, my soul is a witness.

Only through GOD's grace and love one lives –
My soul is a witness.

And with His promise a Heavenly home He gives –
Thank GOD......My soul is a witness!

Prayer Changes Things

You're always in our thoughts and prayers,
For we know **prayer changes things**.

And in our hearts we know GOD cares,
And we know **prayer changes things**.

Though burdens may seem hard to bear,
Don't worry, **prayer changes things**.

Whatever the load, our GOD will share,
Through His promise, **prayer changes things**.

Just be steadfast and never doubt,
Because by faith, **prayer changes things**.

The prayers of the righteous will bring us out,
Have faith in GOD for, **prayer changes things**.

In collaboration with:
Valerie McWashington

GOD Will

When the going gets rough
Remember GOD will

Don't give up when things are tough
Just remember, GOD will

When there's no hope in sight,
You know, GOD will

Even in your darkest night
Just hold on, GOD will

When your friends deceive,
Have faith, GOD will

Just trust and believe,
Hallelujah, GOD will

When your burdens seem too heavy to bear,
Don't worry, GOD will

No one to care and no one to share,
Remember his promise....

GOD will

Every Day Is A Blessing

On Sunday, a day to worship and fellowship,
You are blessed

On Monday, A new week begins for work and for friends,
You are blessed

On Tuesday, a brand new day and new things to do,
You are blessed

On Wednesday, the middle of the week and you're half way through,
You are blessed

On Thursday, beginning to bring most things to an end,
You are blessed

On Friday, last day to work and make plans to begin again,
You are blessed

On Saturday, a day to relax and reflect on what you should do,
You are blessed

Yes, every day is a blessing, for GOD gave each one to you.

Thank GOD, you are blessed!

Letter From A Friend

I just had to write you to tell you how much I love and care for you. Yesterday, I saw you walking and laughing with your friends; I hoped that soon you'd want me to walk along with you, too. So I painted you a sunset to close your day and whispered a cool breeze to refresh you. I waited, but you never called; I just kept loving you.

As I watched you fall asleep last night, I wanted so much to touch you. I spilled moonlight onto your face, trickling down your cheeks, as so many tears have. You didn't even think of me; I wanted so much to comfort you.

The next day I exploded a brilliant sunrise into a glorious morning for you, but you rushed off to work, you didn't even notice. My sky became cloudy, and my tears were the rain.

I love you. Oh, if you'd only listen. I really love you. I try to say it in the quiet of the green meadow and in the blue sky. The wind whispers my love throughout the treetops and spills it into the vibrant colors of all the flowers. I shout it to you in the thunder of the great waterfalls, and compose love songs for birds to sing to you. I warm you with the clothing of my sunshine and perfume the air with nature's sweet scent. My love for you is deeper than any ocean and greater than any need in your heart. If you'd only real-ize how much I care.

My Dad sends his love. I want you to meet him; He cares, too. Fathers are just that way. So, please call me soon. No matter how long it takes, I'll wait, because I love you.

Your friend,

JESUS

Author Unknown

You're Never Alone

It seems we all have our trials and tribulations,
and sometimes we wonder just how we're going to make it.
Our days are long, and our nights are even longer.

It may seem that we've cried so hard, for so long,
until the tears no longer flow.
Our hearts ache and overflow with pain.

Lord, our friends have listened to and shared,
our problems for so long, and we worry that perhaps
we're taking advantage of their love and compassion.

Don't be discouraged, and don't despair. When the
quiet times come and in the darkest of night,
just lift your eyes to heaven, and your hands to GOD,
and know that He will listen and see you through.........

You're Never Alone!

Let Go And Let GOD

When problems surround you on every side,
and you've done all that you could,

Let go and let GOD.

When talking and pleading just fade into thin air
And you've done everything you should,

Let go and let GOD.

When all your hopes and dreams have been lost
and you've tried to save them, no matter the cost,

Let go and let GOD.

Pray for the Lord to see you through
and remove your armor,

He'll fight this battle for you,

Let go and let GOD.

Jesus, I Thank You

For the angel that watches over me
Jesus, I thank you.

For gently waking me from my sleep
Jesus, I thank you.

For giving me the strength to clothe,
feed and care for myself
Jesus, I thank you.

For continuing to be my companion
as I travel through out my day
Jesus, I thank you.

For allowing me to see the curves in the road,
and making them straight
Jesus, I thank you.

For protecting my family and keeping all of us safe
Jesus, I thank you.

Lord, for all these things and so much more

Jesus, I thank you!

God's Most Favorite Time of the Year

God's beautiful pastel flowers
being kissed by the morning dews,

God's majestic trees, once bare, proudly
displaying their magnificent hues.

God's gentle songbirds, chirping
beautifully to greet each day.

God's colorful rainbows, after the gentle rain,
are perfect in every way.

God's beautiful sunlight, beaconing
from a blue sky, so clear.

All let me know, that Spring is God's most
favorite time of the year!

A Morning Prayer

Heavenly Father, I come before you, thanking you for touching me with your mighty finger of love and waking me up this morning. I enter into your courts with thanksgiving and into your gates with praise. Father, I declare that this is truly a day that you have made and I will rejoice in it and be exceedingly glad.

Lord, give me strength and move in me throughout this day, regardless of the circumstances and situations. Help me to operate in the fruit of the Holy Spirit at all times. Even when I feel like losing control of my tongue, I won't because your spirit abounds in me. You said, "I am the light", and to let your light so shine in me. Therefore, I will only speak those words that will bring edification to you and others, and anything that does not, I will cast away from me.

Thank you, Heavenly Father, for being the Messiah in my life! My banner, my shield , and my strength. You are the one who fights all of my battles for me.

Thank you GOD for being all that you are to me. Please continue to bless my home, my family, and friends. Keep them safe from all hurt, harm, and danger. I ask that you please wrap your loving arms of protection around them and let them know that you are GOD, and with you ALL things are possible!

And, my dear Heavenly Father, when all is said and done, I pray that you will give us a home, somewhere in your Kingdom, in Jesus' name.........

Amen

He's Never Failed Me

When I call on GOD, in secret prayer,
He's never too busy, He's always there,
He's never failed me.

When I'm all alone, and friends are few,
I can trust in GOD to see me through,
He's never failed me.

When I've been troubled, and cried all night,
My GOD comes in the morning, and makes things right,
He's never failed me.

When things go wrong, as they often will,
GOD will make them right, if you just be still,
He's never failed me.

So, if your heart is heavy, and you're troubled too,
Trust in GOD, He'll see you through,
He Will Never Fail!!

Heaven's Grocery Store

I was walking down life's highway many years ago, when one day I saw a sign that read, "HEAVEN'S GROCERY STORE". As I got a little closer, the door opened wide and when I came to myself, I was standing inside. I saw a host of Angels, they were standing everywhere. One handed me a basket and said, "My child, shop with care".

Everything a Christian needed was in that grocery store and, all you couldn't carry then, you could come back the next day for more. First, I got PATIENCE, LOVE was in the same row. Further down there was UNDERSTANDING, you need that everywhere you go.

I got a bag or two of WISDOM, and a bag or two of FAITH, I just couldn't miss the HOLY GHOST for it was all over the place.

I stopped to get some STRENGTH and COURAGE, to help me run this race. By now the basket was getting full, but I remembered I needed some GRACE. I didn't forget SALVATION, for SALVATION was free! So I tried to get enough of that to save both you and me!

Then I started to the counter to pay my grocery bill, for I thought I now had everything I needed to do my Master's will.

As I went up the aisle, I saw PRAYER, and I just had to put it in, for I knew when I went outside I would run right into sin.

PEACE and JOY were plentiful, they were on the last shelf. SONGS and PRAISES were hanging near, so I just helped myself.

Then I said to the Angel, "Now, how much do I owe?" He smiled and said, "Just be sure to take them everywhere you go." Again, I smiled at him and said, "How much do I really owe?"

The Angel smiled again and said, "My child, Jesus paid your bill a long time ago."

Author Unknown

Colors of the Rainbow

GOD put the colors in the rainbow,
When He made you and me.

Red, yellow, black and white,
For all the world to see.

These are all GOD's colors,
And we are all the same.

All painted bold and bright,
In His son Jesus' name.

We are all brothers and sisters,
Cut from the same cloth, you see...

And we must all learn to love one another,
The way GOD wants it to be.

Bless all the colors of the rainbow,
A majestic painting in the sky;

Viewed by the world below,
And created by our Lord on high.

Bless This House

Bless this house, dear GOD,
For this shelter, we give thanks.

We humbly thank You for these walls so sturdy.

Thank You for these doors and windows,
together so tight and strong.

For the floors that give us a firm foundation,
and the roof that covers our home, we give thanks.

And Lord, bless this family that abides inside,
protected from the sun, wind and rain…
sheltered by Your love!

Just Ask

With GOD, all things are possible......
Just Ask

No problem is ever too big or too small......
Just Ask

When burdens seem too heavy to bear......
Just Ask

If you feel all alone and helpless......
Just Ask

Heartache and pain that won't go away......
Just Ask

When doors are closed,
and slammed shut in your face......
Just Ask

When your friends are no longer friends......
Just Ask

If trouble seems to always find you......
Just Ask

Yes, with GOD all things are possible,
and you never have to beg......
Just Ask!!

Our Father Loves Us

Our Father loves us,
No matter what we do;
Good or bad, right or wrong,
He always sees us through.

Our Father loves us,
We're his children everyone;
No matter the race or color,
He cares for every daughter and son.

Our Father loves us,
Though as children, we all make mistakes;
In His own image he made us all human'
And He forgives us for Jesus' sake.

Yes, our Father GOD loves us,
And many times we do not obey His will;
As His children, we're often disobedient,
He's GOD our Father, and He loves us still.

GOD Forgives

GOD forgives when we've done wrong…

GOD forgives when we've caused harm…

GOD forgives when we forget to pray…

GOD forgives when we don't obey…

GOD forgives when others don't…

GOD forgives when we think He won't…

GOD forgives when we're not deserving…

GOD forgives even when we don't serve Him…

GOD forgives and showers us with His grace…

GOD forgives, and prepares for us all His heavenly place…

GOD Forgives!!

Faith

Faith, you know, can move mountains,
Faith can make dreams come true;
Faith can make a prince from a pauper,
Faith can make changes in both me and you.

Faith can change the heart of a lion,
Faith can change your darkest night to day;
Faith can calm a raging sea,
Faith can brighten up your way.

Faith can lift your spirits higher,
Faith can open locked doors for you;
Faith can lighten that heavy load, and
Faith in GOD can always see you through.

Love Is

Love is the look on a mother's face,
as she holds her newborn baby.

Love is the look on the parents' faces
as their toddler takes the first step.

Love is the pride on a father's face,
as he watches his child hit that first baseball.

Love is kneeling beside your precious child,
to hear the very first prayer.

Love is watching a beautiful flower grow.

Love is watching a lovely butterfly,
as it struggles from the cocoon.

Love is many things,
and can be seen in many places.

But, most of all......
Love is GOD, and GOD is Love!!!

Sunday Mornings

Sunday mornings, the most sacred day of the week.
Delicious smells from the kitchen let you know that
it's time to rise and get ready for a day of
worshipping GOD......in His house!

A day to fellowship with others, and thank GOD
for the week just passed, for your family and friends,
for your health and strength.

Let us pray, and thank GOD
for Sunday mornings!

Forgive and Forget

When your friends deceive you...
Forgive and Forget.

And your friends just can't be found...
Forgive and Forget.

When your loved ones hurt you...
Forgive and Forget.

And, loved ones disrespect you...
Forgive and Forget.

When your family deserts you...
Forgive and Forget.

And, your family disowns you...
Forgive and Forget.

If you forgive...you must forget.
When you don't forget,

You haven't truly forgiven!

GOD Is Real

When pain and suffering deep down in your heart you feel…
GOD can heal your heart…

GOD Is Real!

When trouble surrounds you, and there is no way out…
Just be still… …GOD will open doors…

GOD Is Real!

When satan sneaks in and tries to make you give up,
And destroys your will…
GOD will move satan out…

GOD Is Real!

Deep down in your heart you will know,
And in your soul you must truly feel…

GOD Is Real!

Don't Forget To Pray

As you rise in the morning to begin your day,
Don't forget to pray.

Traveling to your destination and along the way,
Don't forget to pray.

Take time to reflect on the things you should say,
Don't forget to pray.

As you meet and greet others throughout your day,
Don't forget to pray.

GOD is so easy to talk to, and He's always right there,
Don't forget to pray.

GOD Is Good – All The Time

GOD is good all the time,
Even when we're not deserving.

GOD is good all the time,
It matters not the deeds we've done.

GOD is good all the time,
Though sometimes we even forget to pray.

GOD is good all the time,
Even though, at times, we don't thank
Him for His goodness.

GOD is good all the time,
Though sometimes we may go astray.

GOD is good all the time,
He's better to us than we are to ourselves.

Yes, GOD is good all the time,
Yesterday, today, tomorrow and forever!

F.R.I.E.N.D

F – is for "Forever" a friendship should be…

R – is for "REAL", there's no faking it you see…

I – is for the "Inspiration" we give to one another…

E – is for "Everything" we do for each other…

N – is for "Never" will this friendship end…

D – is for the "Dedication" since our friendship began…

A "FRIEND" is a jewel, and a friendship should be treasured!

Behind The Clouds

Behind the clouds the sun shines,
Though it may be a rainy day.

Behind the clouds there's a rainbow,
As the sun chased the clouds away.

Behind the clouds the skies are blue,
And the day is so clear and bright.

Behind the clouds are the heavens,
Now all clear to welcome the stars at night.

Just Be Still

The Lord will fight your battles,
If you just be still.

In your prayers, ask Him to help you,
And just be still.

Put your hands in GOD's hands,
Hold on and just be still.

Let GOD take His time – He'll work it out,
Just be still.

Tell GOD all about your troubles, trust in Him,
And just be still.

Don't worry, He NEVER fails,
Have faith and just be still!!

If GOD Brought You To It

In life we all have pain to bear,
But no matter how deep the pain,
We know GOD will be there;

Believe – If GOD brought you to it,
He'll walk you through it.

You may have suffered the loss of a loved one,
And felt that your life was over and done;

Be comforted – If GOD brought you to it,
He'll walk you through it.

There have been so many times when you've had to cry,
And you called on GOD to ask Him why;

Have faith – If GOD brought you to it,
He'll walk you through it.

When trouble comes like a thief in the night,
And you don't know how to make things right;

Hold on – If GOD brought you to it,
He'll walk you through it.

Though your entire world seems upside down,
And you feel you won't make it through;
Just call on GOD, He'll step right in,
There is nothing He can't do.

Remember – If GOD brought you to it,
He'll walk you through it.

AMEN!!

GOD Sees All

GOD sees all......
He sees everything we do,
He watches over you and me,
And guides us safely through.

GOD sees all......
From Him we cannot hide,
He sees us when we're doing wrong,
And in His grace we must abide.

GOD sees all......
Whenever we do right He sees,
And this is what He asks of us,
For He is truly pleased.

GOD sees all......
He sees us whether day or night,
He sees though we may cloak and shield,
In GOD's eyes we must do right.

GOD Sees All!!

My Soul is a Witness
Order Form

If you would like to order this book,
please complete the following information.

_____
Name (Please print)

_____
Street Address

_____
City   State   Zip

_____
Phone

Number of books _____ x $ 7.00	=	$ _____
Shipping	=	$ _____
Total Enclosed	=	$ _____
Add $1.00 shipping for each book ordered.		

*** FREE SHIPPING FOR ORDERS OF SIX (6) OR MORE ***

Make check or money order payable to "RIM Books" and mail to:

RIM Books
P.O. Box 311825
Atlanta, GA 30331

You may also make payment at "www.paypal.com"

Please allow 3 to 4 weeks for delivery.
If you have questions regarding your order,
Email address: rimbooks2003@yahoo.com

My Soul is a Witness
Order Form

If you would like to order this book,
please complete the following information.

_____
Name (Please print)

_____
Street Address

_____
City   State   Zip

_____
Phone

Number of books _____ x $ 7.00	=	$ _____
Shipping	=	$ _____
Total Enclosed	=	$ _____
Add $1.00 shipping for each book ordered.		

*** FREE SHIPPING FOR ORDERS OF SIX (6) OR MORE ***

Make check or money order payable to "RIM Books" and mail to:

RIM Books
P.O. Box 311825
Atlanta, GA   30331

You may also make payment at "www.paypal.com"

Please allow 3 to 4 weeks for delivery.
If you have questions regarding your order,
Email address: rimbooks2003@yahoo.com